Using a Computer as a Money-Making Tool: Step by step guide to make money with computer technology

By

Clara Joseph
(Author)

Table of Content

INTRODUCTION

In the present computerized time, where innovation penetrates each part of our lives, the PC remains as a vital instrument that rises above limits, changes businesses, enables people, energizes developments, and opens uncommon doors for creating pay, creating financial wellbeing, accomplishing independence from the rat race, acknowledging desires, and having an effect in the interconnected, serious, and dynamic universe of the computerized economy, markets, and conditions.

This guide plans to demystify the complex scene of utilizing a PC as a strong, flexible, and significant device for making, improving, teaming up, showcasing, adapting, scaling, and prevailing in different areas, ventures, markets, economies, and settings lined up with your inclinations, assets, objectives, values, missions, dreams, open doors, challenges, patterns, developments, disturbances, guidelines, conditions, and yearnings. Whether you're a beginner, devotee, proficient, business person, financial backer, instructor, understudy, or individual looking to saddle the force of PC innovation, this guide fills in as your extensive guide, asset, motivation, buddy, and impetus for setting out on an extraordinary excursion of investigation, trial and error, development, creation, joint effort, development, improvement, achievement, and satisfaction.

All through this aide, we will investigate a bunch of procedures, systems, stages, devices, methods, potential open doors, difficulties, changes, and models that engage you to explore, investigate, try, carry out, make due, enhance, scale, screen, assess, adjust, develop, and gain from different PC based lucrative open doors, techniques, drives, tries, encounters, excursions, and changes. From outsourcing, remote work, content creation, internet business, internet selling, financial planning, exchanging, advanced abilities, preparing, networks, to recurring sources of income, this guide gives noteworthy bits of knowledge.

As we set out on this energizing, testing, fulfilling, satisfying, and extraordinary excursion together, it's crucial to embrace a mentality of interest.

Much obliged to you for setting out on this groundbreaking excursion. May you explore, investigate, analyze, advance, make, team up, market, adapt, scale, and prevail with regards to saddling the force of PC innovation to accomplish your monetary, individual, proficient, and enterprising objectives.

Chapter 1

1.0 Figuring out the Computerized Scene

In the present interconnected world, the computerized scene envelops a huge and dynamic climate that shapes how people, organizations, and associations cooperate, impart, and work. Understanding this computerized scene is pivotal for exploring open doors, difficulties, and patterns that impact different parts of our lives, including trade, correspondence, amusement, instruction, and the sky is the limit from there.

1. Development of the Computerized Scene

The computerized scene has gone through critical changes throughout the long term, driven by mechanical headways, advancements, and changing shopper ways of behaving. From the beginning of the web to the ascent of virtual entertainment, web based business, versatile innovation, and computerized reasoning, the advanced scene keeps on developing, introducing new open doors and difficulties.

2. Key Parts of the Computerized Scene

• Web and Availability: The underpinning of the advanced scene is the web, empowering worldwide availability, correspondence, and admittance to data. The development of high velocity web, versatile organizations, and broadband foundation has worked with consistent cooperation and coordinated effort across borders.

• Advanced Stages and Innovations: Computerized stages, including web-based entertainment, online business, distributed computing, and portable applications, assume an imperative part in molding the computerized scene. These stages empower organizations and people to make, share, and consume content, items, and administrations in creative ways.

• Information and Investigation: Information driven experiences and investigation are basic parts of the advanced scene, enabling associations to figure out customer ways of behaving, patterns, inclinations, and examples. Utilizing information actually can drive direction, improve procedures, and upgrade client encounters.

- Network protection and Security: As the computerized scene extends, network protection and security become basic contemplations. Safeguarding delicate data, getting networks, and alleviating gambles are fundamental to keeping up with trust, respectability, and security in the computerized environment.

3. Patterns Molding the Computerized Scene

- Portable Innovation: The expansion of cell phones, tablets, and wearable gadgets has changed how people access data, impart, shop, and interface on the web.

Portable innovation keeps on driving development, commitment, and availability across different areas.

• Man-made reasoning and Robotization: Propels in man-made brainpower, AI, and computerization are altering the advanced scene, empowering customized encounters, prescient examination, mechanization of undertakings, and streamlining of cycles across businesses.

• Internet business and Advanced Trade: The development of web based business stages, online commercial centers, and advanced installment arrangements has reshaped the retail scene, giving buyers advantageous, consistent, and customized shopping encounters.

• Online Entertainment and Advanced Advertising: Web-based entertainment stages, powerhouse promoting, content creation, and computerized publicizing are changing the way that organizations draw in, associate, and communicate with their ideal interest groups, driving brand mindfulness, dependability, and development.

4. Potential open doors and Difficulties in the Advanced Scene

• Potential open doors: The computerized scene offers immense open doors for advancement, development, cooperation, and change across ventures. Utilizing innovation, information, stages, and computerized procedures can drive upper hand, market extension, client commitment, and income age.

• Challenges: Exploring the advanced scene requires tending to difficulties, for example, contest, network protection chances, information security concerns, administrative consistence, mechanical disturbances, expertise holes, and developing buyer assumptions. Creating key methodologies, risk the executives procedures, and ceaseless learning are fundamental to exploring these difficulties successfully.

Chapter 2

2.0 Outsourcing and Remote Work

As of late, outsourcing and remote work have arisen as unmistakable patterns reshaping the customary business scene. Empowered by innovative headways, changing work societies, and advancing business sector elements, outsourcing and remote work offer adaptability, independence, and open doors for people and associations the same.

This asspect investigates the ideas, advantages, difficulties, and patterns related with outsourcing and remote work in the present advanced age.

1. Understanding Outsourcing and Remote Work

• Outsourcing: Outsourcing alludes to working freely on a legally binding premise, offering types of assistance, abilities, or mastery to clients, organizations, or associations without long haul responsibilities. Consultants frequently work as independently employed people, offering administrations like composition, plan, counseling, programming, promoting, and more to a different scope of clients on an undertaking premise.

•   Remote Work: Remote work includes performing position liabilities, undertakings, or jobs beyond a customary office climate, normally from home, collaborating spaces, or different areas. Remote work game plans influence innovation, specialized apparatuses, and joint effort stages to work with efficiency, network, and commitment among appropriated groups and people.

2. Advantages of Outsourcing and Remote Work

• Adaptability and Independence: Outsourcing and remote work offer people adaptability in picking projects, clients, timetables, and areas. This adaptability permits experts to adjust work, individual life, and expert responsibilities as per their inclinations and needs.

• Admittance to Worldwide Open doors: Outsourcing and remote work empower people to get to a worldwide commercial center of chances, clients, tasks, and coordinated efforts past geological requirements. This admittance to a different scope of clients, businesses, and markets can extend proficient organizations, encounters, and development potential.

•   Cost Reserve funds and Proficiency: Remote work game plans can bring about cost reserve funds for people and associations by diminishing driving costs, office overheads, and functional expenses. Furthermore, remote work can improve efficiency, proficiency, and execution through adaptable workplaces, diminished interruptions, and streamlined work processes.

- Balance between fun and serious activities: Outsourcing and remote work advance balance between serious and fun activities by permitting people to alter their timetables, surroundings, and schedules as per individual inclinations, responsibilities, and obligations. This equilibrium can add to worked on psychological well-being, prosperity, and in general personal satisfaction.

3. Difficulties and Contemplations

- Confinement and Joint effort: Outsourcing and remote work can prompt sensations of disengagement, separation, and absence of cooperation among people and groups. Keeping up with correspondence, association, and cooperation through virtual gatherings, group collaborations, and local area commitment is vital for encouraging connections, cooperation, and culture.

• Self-control and Efficiency: Outsourcing and remote work require self-control, inspiration, and time usage abilities to keep up with efficiency, fulfill time constraints, and convey results. Laying out schedules, defining limits, and focusing on errands can assist people with overseeing time, center, and accomplish objectives actually.

•	Monetary Steadiness and Security: Outsourcing can include vacillations in pay, income, and monetary solidness because of task based work, variable client interest, and financial elements. Fostering an enhanced client base, setting clear installment terms, and overseeing funds wisely can relieve dangers, vulnerabilities, and monetary difficulties related with outsourcing.

4. Future Patterns and Open doors

• Gig Economy and Independent Commercial centers: The gig economy and independent commercial centers keep on developing, giving people admittance to many open doors, stages, and joint efforts across ventures, areas, and markets. Utilizing stages, organizations, and networks can extend reach, perceivability, and development expected in the independent commercial center.

• Remote Work Arrangements and Practices: Associations are taking on remote work strategies, practices, and advances to help disseminated groups, adaptable work plans, and distant coordinated effort. Putting resources into specialized devices, cooperation stages, and remote work systems can upgrade network, commitment, and efficiency among remote groups and people.

• Abilities Advancement and Preparing: Outsourcing and remote work require ceaseless learning, abilities improvement, and preparing to adjust to developing patterns, innovations, and market requests. Putting resources into proficient turn of events, confirmations, and skill can upgrade seriousness, offer, and potential open doors

in the independent and remote work scene.

Chapter 3

3.0 Making and Adapting Content

In the present, content creation and adaptation have become fundamental systems for people, organizations, and associations trying to connect with crowds, fabricate marks, and produce income on the web. With the multiplication of computerized stages, advances, and utilization propensities, making important, pertinent, and convincing substance offers chances to interface with crowds, drive traffic, and adapt content through different channels, methodologies, and models. This part investigates the ideas, best practices, methodologies, and contemplations related with making and adapting content in the computerized scene.

1. Grasping Substance Creation

• Content Sorts and Configurations: Content creation incorporates different sorts, configurations, and mediums, including articles, web journals, recordings, digital broadcasts, infographics, digital books, online classes, courses, virtual entertainment posts, and then some. Distinguishing interest groups, stages, and targets can direct happy creation techniques, subjects, and organizations custom-made to crowd inclinations, interests, and needs.

• Quality and Importance: Making superior grade, pertinent, and important substance is fundamental to connect with crowds, lay out believability, and assemble trust. Reliably creating content that resounds with ideal interest groups, addresses trouble spots, tackles issues, and conveys bits of knowledge, data, or amusement can cultivate associations, connections, and reliability over the long run.

•	Narrating and Marking: Integrating narrating, marking, and personalization into content creation techniques can separate brands, pass on messages, and inspire feelings, encounters, and associations with crowds. Creating genuine, convincing accounts, visuals, and encounters that reflect brand values, voice, and character can upgrade acknowledgment, review, and commitment across stages and channels.

2. Adapting Content Procedures

• Publicizing and Sponsorships: Adapting content through publicizing and sponsorships includes cooperating with brands, promoters, or stages to show advertisements, advance items, or support content in return for income, commissions, or associations. Utilizing promoting organizations, stages, and associations can streamline reach, perceivability, and adaptation open doors for content makers.

• Membership and Participation Models: Executing membership and participation models empowers content makers to adapt content through repeating income, memberships, or premium admittance to select substance, assets, or encounters. Offering layered enrollments, advantages, and motivations can draw in and hold endorsers, allies, and networks around satisfied makers' brands, content, and stages.

• Subsidiary Advertising and Associations: Using associate showcasing and organizations permits content makers to acquire commissions, references, or impetuses by advancing, suggesting, or supporting items, administrations, or brands inside happy, stages, or crowds.

Distinguishing important, legitimate, and adjusted subsidiary projects, items, or partners can upgrade believability, trust, and transformation rates for adaptation methodologies.

•	Internet business and Advanced Items: Adapting content through web based business and computerized items includes selling items, stock, courses, digital books, formats, or advanced resources connected with content, aptitude, or specialty markets. Creating significant, applicable, and top notch items, assets, or contributions can broaden income streams, upgrade offers, and adapt crowds inspired by satisfied makers' skill, experiences, or arrangements.

3. Best Practices and Contemplations

• Crowd Commitment and Input: Connecting with crowds, requesting input, and consolidating experiences, inclinations, or ideas into content creation and adaptation techniques can improve significance, worth, and fulfillment. Building people group, encouraging connections, and paying attention to crowd needs, interests, or concerns can direct happy turn of events, adaptation models, and development techniques after some time.

• Content Improvement and Dispersion: Upgrading content for web indexes, stages, and dissemination channels can expand reach, and commitment with interest groups. Executing Website optimization systems, content advancement, dispersion strategies, and stage explicit accepted procedures can improve discoverability, openness, and execution across computerized scenes.

• Legitimate, Moral, and Consistence Contemplations: Guaranteeing consistence with legitimate, moral, and administrative necessities connected with content creation, adaptation, promoting, associations, information security, and shopper insurance is fundamental to keep up with trust, honesty, and validity with crowds, partners, and specialists. Understanding and complying with important regulations, rules, arrangements, and best practices can alleviate dangers, liabilities, and difficulties related with content adaptation techniques.

Chapter 4

4.0 Internet business and Web based Selling

Web based business and internet selling have altered the retail business, giving organizations, business visionaries, and purchasers with new open doors, stages, and encounters to purchase, sell, and execute labor and products in the computerized commercial center. With the multiplication of web advances, cell phones, and computerization, online business has changed customer ways of behaving, market elements, and plans of action, empowering consistent, helpful, and customized shopping encounters across different areas, ventures, and districts. This part investigates the ideas, methodologies, patterns, and contemplations related with web based business and web based selling in the present computerized age.

1. Grasping Online business

• Internet business Outline: Web based business, or electronic trade, alludes to the purchasing, selling and advertising. Online commercial centers and Online business incorporates different plans of action, including B2C (business-to-shopper), B2B (business-to-business), C2C (purchaser to-customer), and D2C (direct-to-buyer), customized to explicit ventures, crowds, and market sections.

• Online business Stages and Arrangements: Web based business stages, arrangements, and advancements empower organizations to make, make due, and streamline online stores, sites, or commercial centers to exhibit items, process exchanges, and convey worth to clients.

Utilizing web based business, like Shopify, WooCommerce, Magento, BigCommerce, or custom arrangements, can work with consistent combination, adaptability, and customization in view of business needs, goals, and prerequisites.

• Web based business Patterns and Advancements: Internet business patterns and developments, including portable shopping, social trade, increased reality, augmented reality, computer based intelligence (man-made consciousness), chatbots, voice search, omnichannel encounters, membership models, and customized suggestions, keep on reshaping the web based business scene, customer assumptions, and industry rehearses. Embracing innovation, development, and client driven techniques can separate brands, upgrade seriousness, and drive development in the advancing web based business environment.

2. Methodologies for Internet Selling

• Item Determination and Obtaining: Distinguishing, choosing, and obtaining items or administrations in light of market interest, patterns, contest, evaluating, quality, providers, and client inclinations is fundamental to lay out an upper hand, separation, and incentive in the web-based commercial center. Leading statistical surveying, dissecting client experiences, and assessing store network abilities can direct item determination, advancement, and obtaining procedures lined up with business targets and market open doors.

• Valuing and Serious System: Creating evaluating procedures, serious situating, and offers that line up with market elements, client assumptions, item separation, cost designs, and business targets can improve productivity, piece of the pie, and consumer loyalty in the web based selling scene. Carrying out unique evaluating, limits, advancements, devotion projects, and worth added administrations can improve intensity, transformation rates, and client dependability across internet business channels.

• Advertising and Client Securing: Carrying out promoting procedures, strategies, and channels, including Website design enhancement (site improvement), web search tool showcasing, virtual entertainment advertising, email advertising, content advertising, powerhouse associations, offshoot programs, retargeting efforts, and internet publicizing, can drive traffic, commitment, and changes for web based selling drives. Creating focused on, customized, and coordinated promoting efforts across web based business stages, channels, and touchpoints can draw in, secure, and hold clients actually.

•	Client Experience and Fulfillment: Zeroing in on client experience, fulfillment, and accomplishment through consistent, helpful, and customized web based shopping encounters, including easy to understand interfaces, route, item revelation, search usefulness, checkout processes, installment choices, transporting, conveyance, returns, client service, and post-buy associations, is vital for assemble trust, steadfastness, and support among online clients. Upgrading site execution, responsiveness, availability, security, and dependability can improve fulfillment, maintenance, and lifetime an incentive for internet selling drives.

3. Contemplations and Best Practices

• Lawful, Consistence, and Security: Guaranteeing consistence with internet business regulations, guidelines, norms, and best practices connected with purchaser insurance, protection, information security, tax collection, licensed innovation, promoting, installments, transportation, and worldwide exchange is fundamental to alleviate dangers, liabilities, and difficulties related with web based selling drives. Carrying out secure, straightforward, and moral practices across internet business tasks, cycles, and exchanges can encourage trust, certainty, and validity with clients, partners, and specialists.

• Innovation, Joining, and Development: Utilizing innovation, mix, and advancement to streamline online business stages, arrangements, cycles, and encounters in view of arising patterns, advancements, potential open doors, and client inclinations can upgrade seriousness, nimbleness, versatility, and flexibility in the powerful internet business scene. Putting resources into web based business capacities, associations, joint efforts, and environments that line up with business targets, procedures, and development drives can drive advancement, separation, and progress in the developing computerized commercial center.

• Estimation, Examination, and Enhancement: Carrying out estimation, investigation, and streamlining systems, devices, and practices to screen, break down, and further develop web based business execution, measurements, key execution markers, client ways of behaving, patterns, and open doors can illuminate navigation, procedures, and drives to improve benefit, productivity, and viability in internet selling attempts. Creating information driven, bits of knowledge driven, and results-driven ways to deal with web based business estimation, examination, and advancement can upgrade ventures, assets, and results in the cutthroat computerized commercial center.

Chapter 5

5.0 Effective financial planning and Exchanging On the web

Effective money management and exchanging on the web have become progressively well known roads for people, brokers, and financial backers trying to partake in monetary business sectors, resource classes, and amazing open doors through advancements and administrations. With the democratization of access, progressions in innovation, and developing business sector elements, web based money management and exchanging offer comfort, adaptability, straightforwardness, and chances to profit by monetary instruments, techniques, and patterns continuously. The the ideas, techniques, contemplations and patterns related with putting and exchanging on the web in the present interconnected and computerized monetary scene has become much more easier and anyone can take advantage.

1. Grasping Internet Contributing and Exchanging

• Contributing versus Exchanging: Contributing alludes to the drawn out assignment of capital into resources, portfolios, or monetary instruments with the assumption for producing returns, pay, appreciation, or abundance amassing after some time. Interestingly, exchanging includes transient purchasing, selling, or trading of monetary instruments, resources, or positions to benefit from market valuable open doors, changes, patterns, or techniques inside unambiguous time spans, methodologies, and goals.

- Online Stages and Businesses: Web based money management and exchanging stages, businesses, and administrations work with admittance to monetary business sectors, instruments, trades, items, research, devices, investigation, and execution abilities for people, dealers, financial backers, organizations, and counsels. Utilizing on the web stages, for example, money market funds, exchanging stages, robo-counselors, speculation applications, commercial centers, and trades, empowers clients to oversee portfolios, execute exchanges, access data, examine information, and screen execution continuously.

•	Monetary Instruments and Markets: Web based money management and exchanging incorporate many monetary instruments, markets, resource classes, and valuable open doors, including stocks, securities, trade exchanged reserves, shared reserves, choices, prospects, forex (unfamiliar trade), digital currencies, products, records, and that's only the tip of the iceberg. Enhancing portfolios, techniques, and openings in view of hazard resistance, targets, inclinations, economic situations, and ability can improve returns, alleviate chances, and accomplish monetary objectives in the dynamic and serious scene of web based money management and exchanging.

2. Techniques and Approaches

• Risk The board and Distribution: Carrying out risk the executives, broadening, resource allotment, and portfolio methodologies custom fitted to individual objectives, time, risk resistance, monetary conditions, economic situations, and targets is fundamental to explore, make due, and advance internet contributing and exchanging attempts. Creating trained, informed, and information driven ways to deal with risk evaluation, position estimating, resource determination, and technique execution can upgrade execution, flexibility, and maintainability in monetary business sectors.

• Specialized and Major Examination: Using specialized and essential investigation systems, instruments, markers, diagrams, designs, research, news, occasions, and bits of knowledge can illuminate navigation, examination, and procedures connected with web based money management and exchanging exercises. Investigating market patterns, designs, ways of behaving, relationships, instability, force, opinion, essentials, and macroeconomic variables can work with educated, key, and ideal choices across resource classes, markets, and open doors.

•   Exchanging Styles and Time spans: Embracing exchanging styles, time spans, and approaches lined up with individual inclinations, ability, objectives, and economic situations, for example, day exchanging, swing exchanging, position exchanging, scalping, pattern following, energy exchanging, esteem financial planning, development contributing, antagonist contributing, and the sky is the limit from there, can improve execution, consistency, and progress in web based money management and exchanging exercises. Creating abilities, information, experience, and skill in unambiguous styles, procedures, and strategies can upgrade seriousness, dexterity, and versatility in powerful monetary business sectors.

3. Contemplations and Best Practices

• Schooling, Exploration, and Ceaseless Learning: Putting resources into schooling, research, assets, courses, confirmations, classes, online classes, guides, mentors, networks, and stages to upgrade information, abilities, aptitude, and capacities connected with web based financial planning and exchanging is fundamental to explore, adjust, and prevail with regards to advancing business sectors, advancements, guidelines, and open doors. Focusing on nonstop learning, advancement, improvement, and variation to arising patterns, experiences, techniques, apparatuses, and practices can cultivate development and strength in the serious scene of web based financial planning and exchanging.

• Guideline, Consistence, and Morals: Understanding, complying to, and following administrative necessities, regulations, rules, principles, morals, and best works on administering internet contributing and exchanging exercises, businesses, trades, exchanges, items, administrations, exposures, detailing, and tasks is fundamental to moderate dangers, liabilities, challenges, extortion, unfortunate behavior, and results related with monetary business sectors, guidelines, and specialists.

Focusing on straightforwardness, uprightness, responsibility, obligation, and reliability in web based money management and exchanging attempts can encourage certainty, believability, and associations with partners, clients, and controllers.

• Innovation, Security, and Framework: Utilizing innovation, security, framework, stages, organizations, frameworks, programming, apparatuses, conventions, and practices that focus on execution, unwavering quality, accessibility, versatility, productivity, security, secrecy, validation, approval, encryption, consistence, strength, and assurance of resources, information, data, exchanges, characters, and activities is fundamental to guarantee wellbeing, security, dependability, and confidence in web based money management and exchanging conditions. Carrying out strong, secure, and tough innovations, practices, and conventions lined up with industry guidelines, best practices, guidelines, and online protection structures can moderate dangers, weaknesses, breaks, disturbances, and effects related with computerized resources.

Chapter 6

6.0 Computerized Abilities and Preparing

In the present quickly advancing computerized scene, obtaining, creating, and dominating advanced abilities have become fundamental for people, experts, organizations, and associations to flourish, enhance, and prevail in different areas, enterprises, jobs, and conditions. Computerized abilities incorporate a great many skills, information, capacities, instruments, innovations and practices that empower people and associations to use computerized advances, patterns and valuable open doors.

1. Grasping Advanced Abilities

• Computerized Education and Skills: Computerized abilities envelop major, middle, and high level capabilities connected with utilizing and exploring data and content.

• Key Computerized Abilities: Advanced abilities incorporate different regions, areas, and disciplines, including however not restricted to computerized proficiency, data innovation, software engineering, programming, coding, programming improvement, website architecture, client experience plan, network safety, information science, man-made reasoning (artificial intelligence), AI, advanced showcasing, virtual entertainment, content creation, interactive media creation, web based business, internet selling, business venture, development, project the executives, light-footed strategies, remote work, coordinated effort, correspondence, decisive reasoning, critical thinking, innovativeness, versatility, strength, and deep rooted learning.

•   Advanced Change and Development: Computerized abilities empower people and associations to explore, adjust, lead, enhance, change, upset, and prevail in the advanced age by embracing, utilizing, coordinating, improving, scaling, and adapting advancements, patterns, functional efficiencies, upper hands, market disturbances, industry shifts, administrative changes, and cultural effects in different areas, businesses and markets,

2. Significance of Computerized Abilities and Preparing

• Upper hand and Separation: Getting, creating, and dominating computerized abilities give people and associations an upper hand, separation, offer, development capacities, market authority, client commitment, memorability, ability fascination, maintenance, efficiency, productivity, versatility, manageability, strength, and progress.

• Profession Development and Valuable open doors: Putting resources into advanced abilities and preparing improves people's employability, vocation development, amazing open doors, versatility, changes, yearnings, procuring potential, proficient turn of events, organizations, associations, joint efforts, commitments, influence, fulfillment, satisfaction, and outcome in different jobs.

Chapter 7

7.0 Constructing and Adapting On the web Networks

In today's world, constructing and adapting on the web networks have arisen as strong systems for people, organizations, associations, powerhouses, and makers trying to associate, connect with, team up, cooperate, share, learn, develop, and adapt to networks.

Grasping Web-based Networks

• Definition and Attributes: Online people allude to virtual, advanced, social, intuitive, cooperative, and arranged conditions, spaces, places, gatherings, organizations, channels, networks, or where people, clients, individuals, members, crowds, partners, and elements associate, impart, team up, interface, draw in, share, contribute, work together, co-make, talk about, banter, trade, learn, develop, support, impact, motivate, engage, network, have a place, and develop around normal interests, objectives, values, missions, dreams, goals, challenges, encounters, personalities, affiliations and ways of behaving.

- Types and platform: this online arena is suitable to explore and gaining mastery of the usage puts a computer professional in a more vantage position (e.g., Meta (facebook) gatherings, LinkedIn gatherings, Twitter talks, Instagram people group), discussions (e.g., Reddit, Quora, Stack Flood), organizations (e.g., Meetup, Eventbrite), stages (e.g., Strife, Slack), people group (e.g., Patreon, Substack), commercial centers (e.g., Etsy, Shopify), channels (e.g., YouTube, Jerk), spaces (e.g., sites, sites, gatherings), and virtual universes . you can experiment with some of these platforms and gain experience on how to leverage and make more income with them.

•   Advantages and Offer: Building on the web networks gives different advantages, offers, benefits, amazing open doors, effects, results, and changes for people, organizations, associations, powerhouses, makers, crowds, partners, and elements, including yet not restricted to association, commitment, joint effort, connection, correspondence, organizing, relationship building, brand building, notoriety the board, authority foundation, impact creation, crowd development, local area advancement, content creation, sharing, dispersion, advancement, promoting, adaptation, income age, client securing, maintenance, faithfulness, backing, criticism, bits of knowledge, advancement, support, strengthening, learning, development, change, and progress in the computerized world.

2. Methodologies for Building On the web Networks

- Crowd Recognizable proof and Focusing on: Distinguishing, understanding, breaking down, sectioning, focusing on, and drawing in unambiguous crowds, socioeconomics, psychographics, ways of behaving, interests, inclinations, needs, issues, challenges, inspirations, assumptions, encounters, values, missions, dreams and targets.

Gaining mastery of these assets will guarantee an exploration in the world of online consulting which draws you closer to cooperate and private individuals.

Chapter 8

8.0 Automated sources of income

Automated sources of income have turned into a sought-after monetary procedure for people, business visionaries, financial backers, and organizations planning to produce repeating income, enhance pay sources, create financial wellbeing, accomplish independence from the rat race, and make manageable, versatile, and strong revenue streams without dynamic, ceaseless, or huge contribution, exertion, time, assets, or work. The ideas of interconnected universe of money, speculation, business, development, innovation, and advanced economy is a thinking that can be acquired by a business conscious person.

1. Understanding Recurring sources of income

•   Definition and Qualities: Recurring sources of income allude to income, profit, benefits, gains, profits, premium, eminences, rents, profits, capital additions, conveyances, or incomes created from speculations, resources, adventures, organizations, properties, portfolios, items, administrations, scholarly properties, advancements, stages, biological systems, or potential open doors that require restricted, negligible, or no dynamic association, cooperation, mediation, exertion, consideration, the board, oversight, upkeep, or tasks once settled, mechanized, enhanced, scaled, or assigned in different areas, enterprises, markets, economies, and conditions.

• Sorts of Automated revenue: Automated sources of income incorporate different sorts, classes, sources, techniques, models, methodologies including yet not restricted to land ventures (e.g., investment properties), financial exchange speculations (e.g., profits, capital increases), business proprietorship (e.g., establishments, organizations), advanced items (e.g., digital books, courses, programming), associate promoting (e.g., commissions), publicizing (e.g., show advertisements, supported content), memberships (e.g., enrollments, administrations), sovereignties (e.g., books, music, licenses), permitting (e.g., scholarly properties, brands), robotized organizations (e.g., outsourcing, print-on-request), online stages (e.g., YouTube, web journals, web recordings), monetary instruments (e.g., securities, Cds), shared loaning, crowdfunding, eminences, candy machines, mechanized stands, capacity units, ATM machines, hardware rentals, transportation (e.g., rideshare, vehicle rentals), and the sky is the limit from there.

• Advantages and Offer: Recurring sources of income give different advantages, offers, benefits for people, business visionaries, financial backers, organizations, and partners. In accomplishing individual, proficient, monetary, way of life, retirement, heritage, humanitarian, and generational objectives, yearnings, dreams, missions, goals, procedures, and economic conditions.

2. Techniques for Building Automated sources of income

•	Recognize Open doors and Resources: Distinguishing, assessing, exploring, breaking down, choosing, securing, creating, upgrading, scaling, enhancing, and overseeing automated revenue resources.

3. Contemplations and Best Practices

•	Risk The executives and Moderation: Making due, moderating, checking, assessing, evaluating, understanding the pattern of income and taking advantage of the most lucrative ones. This can only be achieved by testing and venturing and you end up with the better ones to is more reliable.

•   Legitimate, Consistence, and Morals: Guaranteeing consistence with regulations, guidelines, norms, and rules. There is no better way to achieve success without being consistent. Practice on a regular basis to achieve mastery choosing from the various ideas presented here.

- Persistent Learning and Variation: Embracing ceaseless learning leads to advancement, when it comes to computers, there are new innovations that foster success, in other words, you have to follow the trend and become updated and implement every learned opportunity.

Chapter 9

9.0 Arranging, Scaling, and Future Development

In the domain of business, business, venture, advancement, innovation, and administration, arranging, scaling, and future development are fundamental parts of business growth, all visionaries who are able to perceive business success in the future always believe in progressive growth pattern.

Figuring out Arranging, Scaling, and Future Development

When you start a business, the next is to aids its growth, but you can't do that without effectively monitoring the pattern of growth of your business. This is a very critical aspect of starting a business and making money and for profit maximization, the PC is a very important tool for a singular access to a world of opportunity of business ventures you can partner with and also support yourself to make money as long as you have the necessary skills, information and knowledge.

CONCLUSION

The computerized age has introduced extraordinary open doors for people trying to setup the force of PC innovation as a worthwhile road for producing pay. This book has meant to demystify this excursion, furnishing perusers with a complete guide to explore the multi-layered scene of online revenue sources, computerized stages, and mechanical developments.

All through this aide, we've investigated a horde of systems, strategies, stages, instruments, and methods that engage people to use their PC abilities, mastery, inventiveness, energy, and desire to make, develop, team up, market, adapt, and scale computerized items, administrations, arrangements, content, networks, organizations, stages, and encounters lined up with their inclinations, assets, objectives, values, missions, dreams, open doors, challenges, patterns, developments, disturbances, guidelines, conditions, and settings.

From outsourcing, remote work, content creation, internet business, internet selling, financial planning, exchanging, advanced abilities, preparing, networks, to automated sources of income, this guide has furnished perusers with noteworthy bits of knowledge, down to earth counsel, best practices, contemplations, open doors, difficulties, changes, and guides to explore, investigate, analyze, carry out, make due, improve, scale, screen, assess, adjust, develop, and gain from different PC based lucrative businesses, procedures, drives, attempts, encounters and excursions.

As you consider the bits of knowledge, it's fundamental to perceive that progress in utilizing a PC as a lucrative apparatus requires devotion, responsibility, discipline, diligence and flexibility.

All in all, this book fills in as an impetus, asset, motivation, and ally for people setting out on the groundbreaking excursion of bridling the influence of PC innovation to produce pay, accomplish independence from the rat race, create financial wellbeing, make esteem, have an effect, add to society, and satisfy yearnings.

www.ingramcontent.com/pod-product-compliance
Lightning Source LLC
Chambersburg PA
CBHW050043260726
48658CB00005B/1739